Contracts (Rights of Third Parties) Act 1999

A Milestone in English Law

Written by Vivian Wineman MA Cantab
Edited by Victor H Vegoda FRICS IRRV FBEng PEng

Number 9 in the "Need to Know" Series

Jointly Published by

Estates Gazette
151 Wardour Street
London W1

and

Lark Productions Limited
PO Box 2933, London N20 9LR

Published February 2001

ISBN Number 1 898383 60 X

Other titles in the "Need to Know" Series:-

Practical Ways to Recover your Debts
A Practical Guide to Residential Surveys
Schedules of Dilapidations; Heave, Demolition & Reconstruction
Draft Your Own Terms of Engagement
Condam – Draft Your Own Safety Plan
Landlord & Tenant Covenants Act, 1995
An Introduction to the Party Wall etc. Act, 1996

Printed by Bell & Bain Ltd., Glasgow

Contents

Contracts (Rights of Third Parties) Act 1999

A Milestone in English Law

INTRODUCTION

Lawyers are not known for their flexibility, legislators even less so. The House of Lords which doubles up as the country's Supreme Court and its second legislative chamber has been described as the best proof of life after death. Nevertheless English law has always prided itself on its flexibility. Although in theory Judges decide cases on the basis of precedents, in practice they have always been able to interpret these authorities in a way which has enabled English Law to evolve over generations. Likewise Parliamentary legislation is not like the laws of the Medes and Persians and is continually being amended and repealed.

Yet these changes are normally effected for specific reasons for instance to give effect to changing social attitudes as in Family or Criminal Law or because of the development of increasingly complex economic organisations as in Business and Consumer Law. It happens far less frequently that Parliament changes the law simply because it believe that its predecessors made a mistake. The Contracts (Rights of Third Parties) Act 1999 which came into force on 11th

November 1999 is one of those infrequent occurrences. Privity of contract which at one time was regarded as being intimately bound up with the fundamentals of English Contract

Law had by the second half of the 20th Century come to be regarded simply as an outmoded mistake. This book is an attempt to describe how the doctrine of privity came to be formulated and accepted in English Law and how subsequently it came to be seen as the cause of injustice as well as inconvenience. It will then seek to illustrate some of the problems which have had to be overcome whenever the law is changed.

I have tried to write in a language accessible to laymen. I found it impossible however to write about contracts without some legal jargon creeping in. For instance when people make a contract they become known as parties to it. As there must be at least two parties to a contract someone who is not a party to a contract is known as a third party. A contract is made up of a promise given by someone either in return for another promise or for an immediate favour such as a payment of money. A person who makes a promise is known as a Promisor and the person to whom it is made is known as a Promisee. I apologise in advance for these and other pieces of jargon. They may make the text less elegant but hopefully not less intelligible.

It only remains for me to thank all those who assisted me on this project and to mention two of them by name - my wife, Naomi, for her encouragement and support and my secretary, Janet, for her boundless patience and tolerance.

CONTRACTS (RIGHTS OF THIRD PARTIES)

ACT 1999

A MILESTONE IN ENGLISH LAW

Chapter 1

Privity of Contract

The rule that only a person who is a party to a contract can acquire any rights or be bound by any obligations under it - privity of contract - is regarded as one of the oldest rules of English contract law. The changes to this rule made by the Contracts (Rights of Third Parties) Act 1999 have been seen by some as striking at a basic principle of English law. The story, however, is much more complex.

What should be enforced and by whom?

The law of contract is about enforcing promises and the two central problems that any system of contract law faces are what promises should be enforced and who should be entitled to enforce them.

Clearly someone who pays a large sum of money for a house in reliance on a promise to transfer it to him should be entitled to enforce that promise. On the other hand few systems of contract law will enforce a frivolous bet.

Gratuitous promises

English law established the principle fairly early that gratuitous promises that is undertakings given for no consideration should not be enforced.

Consideration

Furthermore the consideration must be present or future. A promise to do something in exchange for a favour done in the past was not enforceable. The doctrine of consideration had become settled law by the mid-l6th Century. It was formulated in conclusive terms by Sir Edward Coke one of the great figures of English legal history who was to lead the defence of the common law against the claims of the royal prerogative under the Stuarts. In 1588 *Stone -v- Wythipol* he ruled that "every consideration ... must be to the benefit of the defendant or the charge of the plaintiff".

But who should be entitled to enforce such a promise? Should it be the person to whom the promise was given or should it be any person whom the promise was intended to benefit? For several centuries the Courts hesitated over this question. There is a line of cases where promises were enforced on behalf of third parties. In 1677 for instance a man promised his father that he would pay his sister £1,000 in consideration of the father's not selling a forest. Subsequently the sister who was not a party to the agreement sued to enforce it. She was successful. Similarly in a later case in 1823 the trustees of an infant leased property to a tenant on the basis that he would pay a rent to the infant. It was held that the infant could enforce that contract. On the other hand there is a line of cases which produced contrary results the most notable being a case in 1812 where an individual with an interest in a bank promised to deposit of £30,000 with it to prevent a run on the bank. He failed to deposit the money and when the bank subsequently collapsed he was sued by the depositors. They failed.

Tweddle -v- Atkinson
I B & S 393

The issue was finally resolved in a landmark case in 1861. In this case *Tweddle -v- Atkinson* the fathers of a bride and groom agreed before the wedding that the father of the bride would pay the groom a sum of money. He died and failed to pay and the groom understandably distressed brought an action against the executors of his estate. The attitude of the bride is not known. There was no question that there was an enforceable contract here - after all the groom had actually married the bride and the Courts do not enquire into the adequacy of consideration. There was no question also that if there were a binding obligation on the father of the bride this would be enforceable against his estate. The only question was whether the groom could enforce that obligation in view of the fact that the promise was not made to him but to his father. He failed. One of the judges formulated his judgment on the basis that the groom was "a stranger to the consideration".

Another used the phrase that "consideration must move from the promisee".

Tweddle -v- Atkinson

Was upheld in a long line of cases. Their effect was to base the concept of a contract on that of a bargain, on mutuality of obligation between the parties enforcing it. Effectively contracts were taken out of the realm of ethics and into that of commerce. It is no coincidence that the formulation of this rule coincided with the maturity of the industrial revolution and the triumph of liberal capitalism and laissez faire economics in Britain.

Agents and Agency

Like the clear cut rules of 19th Century physics, however, the rule of privity of contract turned out however to be too simplistic. In the first place many business contracts are not entered into by two parties directly but through agents. The agent may conclude the contract but it is his principal who will want the benefits under it and who will be bound by it. This of course could be dealt with easily by treating the agent as a mere extension of his principal but what if the other party was not aware of the existence of the agency and therefore of the principal? By allowing an undisclosed principal to sue on a contract English law opened a breach in the wall of privity.

Contracts for the benefit of Third Parties

Married Woman's Property Act 1982
and the
Third Parties
(Rights Against Insurers) Act 1930

Again, some contracts by their very nature are made for the benefit of third parties. No one would take out a life insurance policy if his rights under it died with him. Many non-life insurance policies are similarly effected for the benefit of third parties. The solution adopted by English law has been to modify the doctrine of privity in relation to insurance piecemeal by statutes such as the Married Woman's Property Act 1882 and the Third Parties (Rights Against Insurers) Act 1930.

Tenancies

Other contracts whilst not expressly made only for the benefit of third parties nevertheless are useless unless they can benefit under them. Leases are an example. Whilst most flat owners regard their lease as a piece of property, in law technically it is a contract. No one however would buy a flat if they knew that when they came to sell it their buyer would not be able to enforce the landlord's obligations to repair and insure the building. The law has therefore adapted to reflect commercial reality. Not only have a tenant's rights to dispose of a lease and in certain circumstances to extend it been protected by successive Acts of Parliament but successors of the original Tenant and Landlord have been entitled to enforce covenants contained in a lease even though they were not parties to the original document.

Restrictive Covenants

In fact however leases are only an illustration of the general principle that commercial relations relating to property are not adequately protected by the privity rule. If the owner of a piece of land sells part of it in reliance on his buyer's undertaking not to construct a building on that part which would completely devalue the rest of the owner's property he would hardly be well served if he found that his buyer could simply escape the obligation by selling the property to a third party who was therefore not bound by it. It is clear therefore the negative restrictive covenants had to be enforceable against successive owners of properties.

Shareholders

Shareholders in a company are another example. The Memorandum and Articles of Association of a company confer rights and obligations on all its shareholders. This would be valueless if their owners could not ensure that when they sold the shares the purchasers would have similar benefits and obligations. Once again the solution of English law has been piecemeal legislation, Section 14 of the Companies Act 1985 re-enacting earlier legislation provides that the Memorandum and Articles of Association constitute a contract between the shareholders of the company as if it had been signed as a deed by all of them.

Factoring or selling The right to receive income

Again somebody might only be prepared to enter into a contract on the basis that he could assign the benefit - a businessman entering into a contract to supply goods might only be able to do so if he could assign the income stream arising under that contract to his bank. Contracts unless they have a personal element in them or contain a restriction against assignment are therefore fully assignable as soon as they are created. There is no great distinction between saying that when a contract is drawn up only those who are parties to it can enforce it but they are able immediately to add third parties by assignment who can do so as well and saying that third parties can enforce a contract as soon as it is made.

The doctrine of privity has therefore had numerous exceptions. With all the modifications however it has nevertheless long been considered that the concept should be abandoned. It has been criticised in many leading cases by judges in the House of Lords, Court of Appeal and the High Court. Academics have been particularly severe on it. Perhaps the most stringent criticisms however have come from judges in other Commonwealth jurisdictions such as Canada and Australia. As a result privity has been abandoned in those countries. The Law Commission in 1996 recommended that the rule be reformed. Their arguments were:-

Arguments for Reform of the law of Privity Of Contract

1. the rule of privity does not give effect to the intentions of the original contracting parties. If the purpose of contract law is the enforcement of promises given why should it stop short of enforcing those promises when they are given in favour of a third party?

2. injustice . Where the parties to the contract have given a third party a reasonable expectation of benefiting under it on which that third party may have relied to his or her detriment it is unjust that he should not have that benefit. This argument is independent of the previous one because even if the original party's intentions change after they make the contract it is unfair if a third party cannot enforce it.

Beswick -v- Beswick (1967) 2 AER 1997

For example, in the case of *Beswick -v- Beswick (1967) 2 AER 1997* a man contracted to sell his business to his nephew on the basis that the nephew should pay him an annuity for the rest of his life and a reduced annuity to his widow. The nephew paid the annuity until the seller died shortly after but refused to pay the widow. She sued. He claimed that she was a stranger to the contract and therefore could not enforce it. The House of Lords agreed with him that she could not enforce it in a personal capacity although it allowed her specific performance as the administratrix of her husband's estate.

Similarly in *Woodar Investment Developments Limited -v- Wimpey Construction UK Limited [1980] 1 AER 571* the owners of a piece of land agreed to sell it for £850,000 with a further £150,000 to be paid to an independent third party. The Purchasers repudiated the contract and when the Vendors sued for damages argued that no damages were due in respect of the broken promise to pay the third party. The case turned on other points but the House of Lords in its judgement held that the Purchasers were right and that it was high time the law was changed.

3. a mismatch arises. The contract can be enforced by the party to it who has suffered no loss whereas the intended beneficiary who has suffered loss cannot sue. This was illustrated in the case of *Beswick -v- Beswick.*

4. as we have seen the judiciary has sometimes been able to effect a just result by allowing the actual parties to the contract to procure specific performance of it. Apart from the artificiality of this solution specific performance is not an automatically available remedy. Moreover it depends on the co-operation of the party to whom the promise was given which may not be available at the time that the contract may be enforceable. Alternatively the promisee though willing may be unable to sue;

5. commercial impracticality. Far from being the hard nose commercial rule it might once have been thought privity does cause real difficulties in commercial life. Examples given are those where people enter into agreements with contractors for them to carry out work for third parties, often companies within the same group. These could end up by being unenforceable. Similarly the contractor might effect indemnity insurance on his behalf and on behalf of sub-contractors and then find that the insurance company

refused to pay a claim made by the sub-contractors because of lack of privity.

It comes as no surprise therefore both that the rule was heavily criticised in other Commonwealth jurisdictions and also that most member states of the European Union do not have the doctrine of privity of contract. Not only the main civil law countries such as France, Germany, Italy, Austria, Spain, Portugal, Benelux and Greece but even Scotland allows third party enforcement. In 1996 the only member states adhering to a strict rule of privity were therefore England, Wales and Northern Ireland on the one hand and the Republic of Ireland on the other. The need to harmonise commercial law within the European Union was yet another argument for reform. The Law Commission's recommendation was therefore unequivocal and set in motion the process which was eventually to lead to the passage of the Act in 1999.

Chapter 2

As we have seen the Courts showed considerable ingenuity in finding ways to avoid the injustice that could be created by the privity of contract rule. Clearly however a fundamental change in the law was required which could only be produced by legislation. In *Beswick -v- Beswick* Lord Denning thought that he had found the panacea in a rather obscure Section in the Law of Property Act 1925.

Section 56(1) the Law of Property Act 1925

Section 56(1) states that:

A person may take an immediate or other interest in land or other property or the benefit of any condition, right of entry, covenant or agreement over or respecting land or other property although he may not be named as a party to the conveyance or other instrument.

This sounds like a fairly obscure point relating to land law. As frequently happens in the law however the real significance lies in the definitions. The definition Section of the Law of Property Act is section 205 and this states that:

"Property" includes any thing in action, and any interest in real or personal property.

"Conveyance" includes every other assurance of property or an interest therein.

Real property means land, personal property means all other property and a thing in action is a legal right which has value. Interests under a contract, the benefit of a debt, shares and loan stock are all examples of things in action. Surprisingly the legal profession often refers to these by the more archaic French term of choses in action.

By its literal wording therefore the Section was not confined to land but comprised any property including debts, shares, etc, and covered any instrument transferring property not merely a conveyance. Lord Denning therefore argued that Parliament had at a stroke abolished the doctrine of privity of contract. Reading the two Sections literally he was right. When the case came before the House of Lords however their Lordships could not accept that Parliament had in a relatively obscure section in an act to codify the principals of land law abolished such a fundamental principle of contract law.

Passage through Parliament

Reform could only come therefore by explicit legislation. Following the publication of the Law Commission's report in 1996 the Bill was introduced first in the House of Lords where it received its second reading on 11th January 1999. It received its third reading on the 14th June

1999 and passed all the Common's amendments by November 1999. It received the Royal Assent on the 11th November.

The Act came into force on that date but for the first six months it applied only to contracts which specifically incorporated it. It applies to all contracts entered into after 11th May 2000 unless they specifically exclude it. Needless to say it is not retrospective and has no bearing on contracts made before it was passed

When introducing the Bill the Lord Chancellor, Lord Irvine, described privity as *"the rule which senior Judges have criticised more than any other rule of English Contract Law"*. Not surprisingly therefore the Bill enjoyed a fairly smooth passage through both Houses of Parliament.

By the standards of some modern legislation the Act is extremely short consisting merely of ten Sections.

Section 1 sets out the central purpose of the Act. It reads as follows:-

1. Right of Third Party to enforce contractual term

(1) Subject to the provisions of this Act a person who is not a party to a contract (a "third party") may in his own right enforce the term of the contract if:-

(a) the contract expressly provides that he may or

(b) subject to sub-section 2 the term purports to confer a benefit on him.

(2) Sub-section (1)(b) does not apply if on a proper construction of the contract it appears that the parties did not intend the term to be enforceable by the third party.

(3) The third party must be expressly identified in the contract by name, as a member of a class or as answering a particular description but need not be in existence when the contract is entered into.

(4) This Section does not confer right on a third party to enforce the term of a contract otherwise than subject to and in accordance with any other relevant terms of the contract.

(5) For the purpose of exercising his right to enforce a term of the contract there shall be available to the third party any remedy that would have been available to him in an action for breach of contract if he had been a party to the contract (and the rules relating to damages, injunctions, specific performance and other relief shall apply accordingly).

(6) Where a term of a contract excludes or limits liability in relation to any matter references in this Act to a third party enforcing the term shall be construed as references to his availing himself of the exclusion or limitation.

(7) In this Act in relation to a term of a contract which is enforceable by a third party - "the promisor" means the party to the contract against whom the term is enforceable by the third party and "the promisee" means the party to the contract by whom the term is enforceable against the promisor.

As can be readily seen Section 1 sets out two conditions each on its own sufficient to enable a third party to enforce a term in a contract. The first is if the contract specifically provides that he is to have the benefit of that term. This is directed at situations like the one which arose in *Beswick -v- Beswick* or in *Woodar Investment Development Limited -v- Wimpey Construction (UK) Limited.* These are extreme cases but also straightforward ones where the rationale for one of the parties entering into the contract was precisely that a third party should have the benefit of its terms. These can now be enforced by the third party with no need for any legal ingenuity.

The other sufficient condition is if a contract purports to confer a benefit on the third party. In this case there is no express term in the contract but the contract's clear intention is to confer a benefit on the third party. Section 1(2) makes the obvious exclusion that if on a proper interpretation of the contract it is apparent that it was not intended by the parties that he should actually be able to enforce it then he cannot rely on the Act even though the contract confers a benefit on him.

Sub-section 3 immediately proceeds to cut down the scope of the Act drastically by limiting the class of third party beneficiaries who can enforce it. This brings us back to the central problem we encountered in Chapter 1. Should any one without restriction be able to enforce a promise regardless of who he is or his relationship to the promisor? While doing away with privity the legislature were not prepared to go to this other extreme and enable promises to be enforced by people of whom the promisor had not even thought and could not even contemplate at the time that the contract was made.

The policy of this sub-section therefore is to ensure that people who can enforce a contract must be clearly identifiable. The third party must therefore be expressly identified in one of three ways either first by name or second as a member of a class or third as answering a particular description.

The first category needs little explanation. In *Beswick -v- Beswick* for instance the wife was clearly identified by name in the contract which would now be enforceable by her without difficulty. The second category again is easily understood. If X pays money to Y in reliance on Y's promise to look after a class of people dear to X such as his children this is now enforceable by them even if they are not all named. The third category takes the second category a little further so that beneficiaries who in ordinary terms would not be seen as belonging to a class but are clearly described can therefore enforce a contract.

The sub-section goes on to say that the person need not exist at the time that the contract is made. A promise to pay an annuity to someone's unborn children or to a future spouse or even to work for a company to be incorporated in the future will therefore be enforceable.

Sub-section 4 effectively clarifies Sub-section 1 making the third party's right of enforcement subject to the general terms of the contract. Clearly the third party is not going to have a better right to enforce a contract than the people who actually entered into it. Sub-section 4 however does go a little further in that it opens the way for the parties to the contract to prescribe the way in which the third party can enforce it and to put limitations on that right of enforcement. They can, for instance, require the contract to be enforced by arbitration rather than litigation or limit the extent of damages which the third party can recover.

Sub-section 5 however clarifies matters in the other direction in that it enables the third party to use all the remedies which would have been available to him as if he had actually been a party to a contract. To a certain extent this is to eliminate one of the problems which the Law Commission had identified with the old rule of privity of contract namely that person to whom the promise under the contract had been made had to apply for specific performance i.e. go to the Court for an order requiring the person to carry out the contract rather than simply obtain damages for his failure to do so. The problem here is that specific performance as an equitable remedy is not available in every situation where damages would be. The problem of the mismatch of remedies is therefore solved.

Sub-section 6 extends the effect of Sub-section 1 so that not only can third parties rely on the Act to enforce the contract but they can also rely on the Act to protect them. This is the flip side of Section 1. In the same way as a main contractor might want all his sub-contractors to have remedies against an employer similarly he may want to limit the employer's remedies against them. The legislation in all these cases is only looking to improve the position of third parties. It is quite common in agreements for parties to limit their liabilities under the common law and they may wish such limitation to extend to third parties such as their agents or sub-contractors. There was a line of cases which cast doubt on a third party's ability to take the benefit of such limitation although the Courts have frequently, as in the case known as the *Eurymedon,* upheld exemption clauses for the benefit of a third party. This doubt is now ended.

Sub-section 7 contains two definitions. As most commercial lawyers will acknowledge providing clear and comprehensive definitions is often the key to effective drafting. The unpredictable possibilities that can be created by extravagant definitions are illustrated by Lord Denning's suggestions in *Beswick -v-Beswick.* Here however the definitions are straightforward and obvious.

Chapter 3

Renegotiation of Contracts

Not surprisingly although the case for reform may be overwhelming, once the process of reform has started new problems emerge. One of these was the extent to which the rights of third parties can be affected by subsequent variations or re-negotiations of a contract. It is obvious that as between the parties to a contract themselves there must be total freedom to amend or re-negotiate its terms. If therefore the parties could not re-negotiate the terms of the contract to the detriment of a third party he could end up being in a stronger position even than the party to whom the promise was actually given. On the other hand, unlimited freedom to re-negotiate the contract could work injustice if the third party could have no confidence that the contract would remain in force.

There was a general consensus therefore when the Bill was formulated that the freedom of contract giving the original parties to it the right to cancel or vary it should be preserved but there should be a cut off point after which the contract could not be cancelled or varied without the consent of the third party. The difficulty was in defining that cut off point. Section 2 addresses that difficulty.

It provides that: -

"2(1) Subject to the provisions of this Section where a third party has a right under Section 1 to enforce a term of the contract then the party to the contract may not, by agreement, rescind the contract, or vary it in such a way as to extinguish or alter his entitlement under that right, without his consent if -

(a) the third party has communicated his assent to the terms to the promisor

(b) the promisor is aware that the third party has relied on the term, or

(c) the promisor can reasonably be expected to have foreseen that the third party would rely on the term and that the third party has in fact relied on it."

Two Tests

We therefore have two tests, one which relates to communication of assent by the third party and the other which relates to reliance by him on the term of the contract. As regards communication of the assent, Section 2(2) reads as follows:-

"(2) The assent referred to in Sub-section (1)(a) -

(a) may be by words or conduct, and

(b) if sent to the promisor by post or other means, shall not be regarded as communicated to the promisor until received by him."

Assent need not be in writing

Service of notice of assent Is effected when received

It is a general legal principle that assent need not be in writing. In fact it does not need to be articulated at all but can be inferred from the third party's conduct. Mere assent however is insufficient. The third party must actually communicate his assent to the promisor. As can be seen, sub-section 2(b) requires that the promisor must actually be made aware of the assent. This reverses the general rule whereby service of documents by post is effected when the document is posted. Here the document containing the assent must actually be received.

Promisor bound if Third Party has Relied on promise

Similarly, the third party's rights under the contract will crystallise if he has actually relied on it. This is a stronger condition than mere assent. It is not necessary therefore that the reliance is communicated to the promisor. The promisor can be bound if he was either aware of the reliance or if he could reasonably be expected to have foreseen that the third party would rely on the contracted term. In both these tests therefore it is essential that the third party has become aware of the existence of the term and has relied on it.

The promisor will be bound if he was aware of that or ought to have been aware in all the circumstances.

Right of Parties to Vary their contract

What then of freedom of contract? This is preserved by Sub-section (3) which provides that: -

"(3) Sub-section (1) is subject to any express term of the contract under which -

(a) the parties to the contract may by agreement rescind or vary the contract without the consent of the third party, or

(b) the consent of the third party is required in circumstances specified in the contract instead of those set out in Sub-section (1)(a) to (c)."

This enables parties to a contract to preserve their right to vary it irrespective of the rights of third parties or alternatively to specify different criteria for the crystallisation point from those specified in the Act.

Section 2 continues as follows: -

"(4) Where the consent of the third party is required under Sub-section (1) or (3) the Court or Arbitral Tribunal may, on the application of the parties to the contract, dispense with his consent if satisfied -

(a) that his consent cannot be obtained because his whereabouts cannot be reasonably ascertained, or

(b) he is mentally incapable of giving his consent.

(5) The Court or Arbitral Tribunal may, on the application of the parties to a contract, dispense with any consent that may be required under Sub-section (1)(c) if satisfied that it cannot reasonably be ascertained whether or not the third party has in fact relied on the terms.

(6) If the Court or Arbitral Tribunal dispenses with the third party's consent, it may impose such conditions as it thinks fit, including a condition requiring the payment of compensation to the third party.

(7) The jurisdiction conferred on the Court by Sub-sections (4) to (6) is exercisable by both the High Court and a County Court."

Whilst this does enable people who get legal advice when they enter into contracts to protect their position to re-negotiate them in the future, it is not so helpful for those less fortunate who enter into contracts and only afterwards discover that they might want to vary them. Part of the rationale for the Act was that people who did not have the benefit of the best legal advice were likely to fall into traps under the old law. Sub-section 4 is designed therefore to remedy this situation by enabling the Court to dispense with the consent of the third party in circumstances where it cannot reasonably be obtained either because he himself cannot be located or if located is incapable of actually giving the consent. Similarly the Court can dispense with the consent if it cannot reasonably ascertained whether the third party has in fact relied on the term. It is important to realise that these decisions by the Court envisaged in Sub-sections 4 and 5 can only be made if both the parties to the contract actually apply to the Court. It is to a certain extent the parties who have themselves agreed to confer the benefit on the third party who wish to restrict or eliminate that benefit and not surprisingly it was felt that the Court should enable them to do so. The term "Arbitral Tribunal" has been introduced as a result of the Arbitration Act 1996 which is discussed in more detail in Chapter 7. Arbitral Tribunal means any body carrying out an arbitration which can in practice consist of one or more arbitrators.

When framing the test of reliance two options presented themselves, either that there should simply be reliance or that the reliance should be to the detriment of the third party. The latter alternative was rejected on the basis that the policy of the Act was to protect the expectations of third parties not give them simply an extra right analogous to the rights that they may already have under the law of tort.

There was some hesitation over the question of the acceptance test. On balance however it was felt that if a third party had become aware of a term of the contract and had accepted it and communicated that acceptance to the promisor then if he wanted to enforce the term he should not have to submit to the further test of having to show that he had actually relied on it.

Chapter 4

Once it has been provided that a third party should be entitled to enforce a contractual term made for his benefit, and once we have defined the circumstances under which he is able to do so, we next have to consider the other side of the coin, namely what defences would be available to the promisor in an action brought by a third party.

Section 3 of the Act reads as follows: -

"3. Defences etc available to promisor

(1) Sub-sections (2) to (5) apply when in reliance on Section 1 proceedings for the enforcement of a term of a contract are brought by a third party.

(2) The promisor shall have available to him by way of defence or set-off any matter that: -

> *(a) arises from or in connection with the contract and is relevant to the term and*
>
> *(b) would have been available to him by way of defence or set-off if the proceedings had been brought by the promisee.*

(3) The promisor shall also have available to him by way of defence or set-off any matter if: -

(a) an express term of the contract provides for it to be available to him in proceedings brought by the third party and

(b) it would have been available to him by way of defence or set-off if the proceedings had been brought by the promisee.

(4) The promisor shall also have available to him: -

(a) by way of defence or set-off any matter and

(b) by way of counterclaim any matter not arising from the contract that would have been available to him by way of defence or set-off or as the case may be by way of counterclaim against the third party if the third party had been a party to the contract.

(5) Sub-sections (2) and (4) are subject to an express term of the contract as to matters that are not to be available to the promisor by way of defence, set-off or counterclaim.

(6) Where in any proceedings brought against him the third party seeks reliance on Section 1 to enforce a term of a contract (including, in particular, a term purporting to exclude or limit liability), he may not do so if he could not have done so (whether by reason of any particular circumstance relating to him or

otherwise) had he been a party to the contract."

Hardly stirring stuff. Indeed, a casual reader might be forgiven for thinking that the taxpayer was not getting full value for money from the efforts of the legislators. In fact, Parliament was using the language of the Law Commission when framing these sections and the wording is attempting to deal with very real problems which can arise in practice.

Definitions

To explain this, we must clarify some terms: -

Defence

"Defence" is a very broad term at law meaning anything which would enable the promisor to say that the contract either had not been made at all or, if made, was not valid, or, if valid, should not be enforceable perhaps because of a breach on the part of the promisee or the non-occurrence of an event which was a prior condition for the promisor's being liable.

Set-off

"Set-off" is where the promisor claims that, whilst he may be liable to the Claimant for monies, the Claimant is also liable to him, usually as a result of the same transaction. An example of a set-off might be a tenant resisting an action for rent by his landlord and claiming that the landlord is liable to him for damages for failing to repair the structure of the building.

Counterclaim

"Counterclaim" on the other hand is much broader in that it need not arise out of the same transaction as the original claim. The only restriction is that the trial of both the claim and counterclaim together must not cause embarrassment, delay or inconvenience. Moreover, a counterclaim can in fact exceed the amount of the claim, which a set-off cannot.

The Law Commission considered the various amendments which have been made by other common law jurisdictions, such as Australia, the United States and New Zealand. They concluded that there were three options for defining a promisor's rights in the event of a claim by a third party.

The first option would be to say that the third party's claim would be subject only to the defences which affected the existence or validity of the contract or the particular contractual provisions which he was looking to enforce. Therefore, set-offs or counterclaims which the promisor could set up against the promisee would not be available to the promisor in an action against him by the third party.

Promisor's rights

The second option would be that the third party's claims would be subject to any defences, set-offs and counterclaims provided that they arose from or in connection with the contract and provided that they would have been available in an action brought by the promisee.

The third option would be that the third party's claim would be subject to all defences, set-offs and counterclaims which would have been available in an action by the promisee, whether or not these had any connection with the contract.

It is easy to see that the first option was too narrow. Effectively, a promisor could claim that the contract had been induced by fraud or mistake or was against public policy, but would not, for instance, be able to bring into account the conduct of the promisee during the course of the contract. To cite just one example, if A sells goods to B, which turn out to be partially defective, B might seek to affirm the contract but look for a price reduction or set-off for damages for defective goods. This is perfectly reasonable and would be enforceable under general law. If, however, A sells goods to B relying on B's promise to pay C the usual format, for instance, of a purchase by credit card, and the goods turn out to be defective, then under the first option B could not claim set-off against A in an action being brought by C.

On the other hand, the third option was regarded as too wide. The third party is not simply stepping into the shoes of the promisee. He has an independent right as the contract was made for his benefit. Moreover, the promisor may have a whole range of counterclaims against the promisee of which the third party may not be aware and of which he may not have been aware when, for instance, he relied on the contract.

The Law Commission therefore settled for the second option which was, incidentally, that favoured by New Zealand when it abolished privity of contract in 1982. The rule itself is set out in Sub-section 2. This provides that the promisor may use any defence or set-off (but not counterclaim) as long as it arises in connection with the contract and is relevant to the term which the third party is looking to enforce. Moreover, it must be a defence or set-off which would have been available to the promisor in proceedings being brought by the promisee.

In line with the general intention of the Act that leaves parties free to make their own contract, Sub-section 3 also provides that, if the parties expressly agree in the contract, then the promisor can have defences against an action by the third party even if they do not arise from the contract. The only proviso is that these remedies etc must be available against the promisee. Effectively, therefore, A can promise to B that, because of some service or consideration rendered to A by B, A will give some benefit to C, but that promise is only to be enforceable by C if B himself could have enforced it.

Promisor's claim Against the Third Party

Sub-section (4) looks at a different problem. What happens if, for instance, as a result of the conduct of the third party, the promisor has a claim against him, which he would not have had against the promisee? If, for instance, the third party himself had committed some fraudulent act against the promisor, then this should be available as a defence. Sub-section (4) therefore states that, where such a defence is available to the promisor against the third party, he should be entitled to plead such defence. Any defence or set-off is available.

Counterclaims, however, are only available if they do not arise from the contract. The principle here being that a third party should not be subjected to a counterclaim for greater than the amount of the contract as a result of a provision designed to protect him.

In line with the general principle of contractual freedom, which is after all the principle which the Act is designed to uphold, Sub-Section 5 enables the parties, in certain express terms, to limit the matters available to the promisor by way of defence etc.

Contracts limiting The liability of Third Parties

Sub-section 6 is designed to cover a very different situation. Parties can enter into a contract limiting the liability of third parties. Strange though this might sound, it is a common procedure in commercial practice. A building contractor in his contract with his client or employer may provide that a sub-contractor's liability should be limited to certain circumstances or to certain sums of money. The sub-contractor is therefore a third party to this contract and may wish to take advantage of its terms in proceedings brought against him in tort by the employer. The effect of the Act is that he can do this. Sub-section 6 imposes a restriction however so that a third party can only use such a defence if it would have been available to him had he been a party to the contract. If the contract for instance were void because of fraud on the part of the promisee, then the third party cannot plead the contract as a defence. Similarly, if quite independently of the promisee, the third party has committed some fraud, he would not be able to use the contract as a defence.

It can be seen therefore that, although the wording of this Section seems rather obscure, it is designed to deal with very real commercial situations.

Chapter 5

Sections 4 and 5 of the Act deal with the question of double liability. Effectively, the Act has opened the door to a new claim by the third party to enforce the contract. Where does that leave the promisee in respect of the same contract?

Section 4 provides that: -

"4 Enforcement of contract by promisee

Section 1 does not affect any right of the promisee to enforce any term of the contract."

Section 5 provides that: -

"5 Protection of party promisor from double liability

Where under Section 1 a term of a contract is enforceable by a third party and the promisee has recovered from the promisor a sum in respect of: -

(a) The third party's loss in respect of the term, or

(b) The expense to the promisee of making good to the third party the default of the promisor, then, in any proceedings brought in reliance on that section by the third party, the court or arbitral tribunal shall reduce any award to the third party to such extent as it thinks appropriate, to take account of the sum recovered by the promisee."

Right of Promisee to enforce contract

One of the intentions of the Act was to enable third parties to enforce provisions made for their benefit so as not to require the Courts to go through the legal gymnastics of making the promisee do so. The Law Commission, however, had no hesitation in recommending that the promisee should still retain his right to enforce the contract even though the third party was now able to do so. After all, the promisee was the person who actually obtained the grant of that right in the first place.

Double Jeopardy

On the other hand, it is equally obvious that the promisor should not be subject to double jeopardy.

Sub-section 5 therefore provides that any award given to a third party must be reduced to take into account any sums recovered by the promisee.

The concern here was for cases where, for instance, a company obtains credit from a supplier on the strength of a guarantee given by its bank and the bank then takes a separate covenant from the company to pay the debt. In such a case in 1842, the guarantor sued the debtor on his covenant to pay. The debtor appealed since the guarantor had not actually been called upon to pay under the guarantee. It was held that the debtor was liable to make payment, although he did have an equitable right that any sums paid to the guarantor should be applied in discharge of his debt to the third party. The Law Commission were unhappy that debtors should have to rely on such a vague equity. It was therefore decided to make it explicit that, in such circumstances, any sums which they had paid out to the promisee, i.e. in this case to the party giving the guarantee, should reduce their liability to the third party.

One Third Party Beneficiary cannot Release Promisor From obligations to Other Third Parties

A separate problem arises when the promisor had effectively given promises to more than one third party. Would one of the third parties be able to release him from his entire promise? The Law Commission considered that the answer to this problem was sufficiently clear that it did not actually need to be put in the legislation. Where there is effectively one obligation owed by the promisor to which there are two beneficiaries, e.g. A undertakes to B to transfer some property into the joint names of C and D, then a release by either C or D discharges A from his obligations. Where, however, it is not a single obligation, but there is more than one obligation, such as an undertaking from A to B that he will pay £100.00 to each of C and D, then, for obvious reasons in those circumstances, a release from C will not discharge A from his obligation to D and vice versa.

Chapter 6

When passing the new Act, Parliament had to ensure that it fitted into existing legislation. The need to protect third party rights had been recognised long before in relation to particular situations which had therefore been addressed by specific provisions tailored to their requirements. To prevent confusion and overlap, these provisions were therefore excluded from the scope of the Act.

Section 6 deals with these. It reads as follows:-

"Section 6 Exceptions:

(1) Section 1 confers no rights on a third party in the case of a contract on a bill of exchange, promissory note or other negotiable instrument.

(2) Section 1 confers no rights on a third party in the case of any contract binding on a company and its members under Section 14 of the Companies Act 1985.

(3) Section 1 confers no right on a third party to enforce –

(a) any term of a contract of employment against an employee.

(b) any term of a worker's contract against a worker (including a home worker) or

(c) any term of a relevant contract against an agency worker.

(4) In Sub-section (3): -

(a) "contract of employment", "employee", "worker's contract" and "worker" have the meaning given by Section 54 of the National Minimum Wage Act 1998

(b) "homeworker" has the meaning given by Section 35(2) of that Act,

(c) "agency worker" has the same meaning as in Section 34(1) of that Act and

(d) "relevant contract" means a contract entered into, in a case where Section 34 of that Act applies, by the agency worker accepting work falling within sub-section 1(a) of that Section.

(5) Section 1 confers no rights on the third party in the case of: -

(a) a contract for the carriage of goods by sea or

(b) a contract for the carriage of goods by rail or road or for the carriage of cargo by air, which is subject to the rules of the appropriate industrial transport convention, except that a third party may, in reliance on that section, avail himself

of an exclusion or limitation of liability in such a contract.

(6) In sub-section (5) "contract for the carriage of goods by sea" means a contract of carriage: -

(a) contained in or evidenced by a bill of lading, seaway bill or a corresponding electronic transaction or

(b) under or for the purposes of which there is given an undertaking which is contained in a ship's delivery order or a corresponding electronic transaction.

(7) For the purposes of sub-section (6): -

(a) "bill of lading", "seaway bill" and "ship's delivery order" have the same meaning as in the Carriage of Goods by Sea Act 1992 and

(b) a corresponding electronic transaction is a transaction within Section (1)(5) of that Act which corresponds to the issue endorsement, delivery or transfer of a bill of lading, seaway bill or ship's delivery order

(8) In sub-section (5), the "appropriate international transport convention" means: -

(a) in relation to a contract for carriage of goods by rail, the

Convention which has the force of law in the United Kingdom under Section 1 of the International Transport Conventions Act 1983,

(b) in relation to a contract for carriage of goods by road, the Convention which has the force of law in the United Kingdom under Section 1 of the Carriage of Goods by Road Act 1965, and

(c) in relation to a contract for carriage of cargo by air: -

(i) the Convention which has the force of law in the United Kingdom under Section 1 of the Carriage by Air Act 1961 or

(ii) the Convention which has the force of law under Section 1 of the Carriage by Air (Supplementary Provisions) Act 1962 or

(iii) either of the amended Conventions set out in Part B of Schedule 2 or 3 to the Carriage by Air Acts (Application of Provisions) Order 1967.

Bills of Exchange Act 1882

As indicated, this Section is dealing with contracts where third party rights already exist. Bills of exchange of which cheques are the best-known example being so widely used in commerce, are the first and obvious exception. Since the 19th Century, the law has protected third parties who acquire bills of exchange. Such bills would be useless if the person to whom a bill of exchange was given could not sell it onto another party. For him to be able to do so, that third party must be able to enforce the bill. The circumstances under which the bill is enforceable are very precisely set out in the Bills of Exchange Act 1882. To have made bills of exchange subject to the new Act would simply have introduced a great deal of uncertainty.

Section 14 of the Companies Act 1985

Similarly, as has already been mentioned, company law contains a framework to protect third party rights, currently embodied in Section 14 of the Companies Act 1985 which re-enacts previous legislation to the same effect. There was no need therefore to give shareholders any further protection.

Where a third party has no rights at all

Sub-section (3) deals with a much more serious exception. Whereas in Sub-sections (1) and (2), the third parties have existing rights which the legislature did not wish to confuse by the creation of new concurrent rights, Sub-section (3) deals with the situation where a third party has no rights at all. It is, of course, not open to a third party to bring any action against an employee for breach of his employment contract. If it were, then, in theory, customers of a company whose workers had gone on strike would be able to bring an action against them. No Government has ever contemplated a situation which would leave workers carrying out industrial action vulnerable to legal action from anyone other than their employer, and not even New Labour would dare to change this. Similarly, the policy of the Act has been to exclude s and home workers as defined by the 1998 Act, which gave effect to the Government's election manifesto proposals on wages.

Contracts for the carriage of goods by sea, railroad or air

Sub-section (5) excludes contracts for the carriage of goods by sea, railroad or air. Transport by sea was covered by the Carriage of Goods by Sea Act 1992. There was no point therefore in having this issue dealt with in the present Act. It is interesting to note the difference between the two Acts. In the 1992 Act Parliament provided that the subsequent holder of a bill of lading became entitled to enforce it but also became subject to all the obligations of the original contractor under the bill of lading. On the other hand the carrier ceased to have any liability to the original contracting party. From the point of view of a promisor both these points put him in a much better position than he would be under the 1999 Act.

As regards the carriage of goods by road or rail or cargo by air these are governed by various international conventions that Parliament has enacted into English Law. Sometimes these conventions require a third party wanting to enforce contracts to assume the burden of a contract. Similarly the conventions sometimes limit the third parties who can taken the benefit of a contract. If the new Act could affect such contracts it would just give rise to confusion. The Law Commission therefore decided the simplest thing was to exclude these matters in the scope of the Act.

Chapter 7

There remained a significant loose end to be wrapped up. The last century has seen an erosion of the principle of freedom of contract. In particular, a number of statutes and statutory instruments have been passed, which restrict a promisor's ability to evade the consequences of his failure to perform a contract. Thus wide-ranging exclusion clauses have been struck down. In the main, these provisions are designed to protect consumers who were perceived as being in a weaker bargaining position particularly when dealing with standard form contracts prepared by traders. In such cases the individual terms may not have been negotiated or even considered by the consumer at the time that the contract was made.

The Unfair Contract Terms Act 1977 went further. Section 2(1) of that Act prevents a promisor relying on a term excluding liability for negligence causing personal injury or death. Section 2(2) prevents him relying on a term excluding liability for any other loss or damage except insofar as the term satisfies the requirement of reasonableness. The question confronting the Law Commission was whether a promisor should be prevented from restricting his liability to a third party in the same way. Like all the questions posed by the Act, this could be answered in a number of ways. The general conclusion was that a third party should not be given the same protection as the person to whom the promise was made in the first place.

Section 7 provides that: -

"(1) Section 1 does not affect any right or remedy of a third party that exists or is available apart from this Act.

(2) Section 2(2) of the Unfair Contract Terms Act 1977 (restriction on exclusion etc of liability for negligence) shall not apply where the negligence consists of the breach of an obligation arising from a term of a contract and the person seeking to enforce it is a third party acting in reliance on Section 1.

(3) In Sections 5 and 8 of the Limitation Act 1980 the references to an action founded on a simple contract and an action upon a specialty shall respectively include references to an action brought in reliance on section 1 relating to a simple contract and an action brought in reliance on that section relating to a speciality.

(4) A third party shall not, by virtue of section 1(5) or 3(4) or (6), be treated as a party to the contract for the purposes of any other Act (or any instrument made under any other Act)."

Section 7(1) is largely formal. The Act is designed to protect third parties and extend their rights. In no way, therefore, should their existing rights be prejudiced. Whilst it would be hard to argue that anything in the Act could have that effect, nevertheless it was considered advisable to spell this out – as the lawyers would put it, "for the avoidance of doubt".

Unfair Contract Terms Act 1977

Sub-section (2) prevents a third party from invoking Section 2(2) of the Unfair Contract Terms Act 1977. This sub-section was the result of considerable deliberation by the Law Commission. Fundamentally, the 1999 Act and the Unfair Contract Terms Act 1977 have contradictory aims. The 1999 Act is designed to give effect to the intentions of contracting parties. For this reason, it is open to the parties to exclude it or modify its application at will. The Unfair Contract Terms Act 1977 by contrast was designed to override the declared intentions of the parties to a contract in order to do justice between them. To extend its basis to third parties would cut across the basis of the reform being effected by the 1999 Act. Moreover, the purpose of the 1999 Act was never to put third parties in the same position as the promisee but simply to ensure that they got those benefits - and only those benefits - intended for them by the parties to the contract. Besides, applying the test of reasonableness to contracting parties was hard enough but, if third parties were to be involved, it would become harder still.

Nevertheless, the Law Commission did not exclude the Unfair Contract Terms Act 1977 entirely. Section 2(1) of that Act can be invoked by third parties.

Negligence causing personal injury or death besides being, hopefully, quite rare, is also sufficiently serious that it should not be possible to exclude liability, even to third parties.

Sub-section (3) clarifies the position that the time limits for an action by a third party are the same as those for the promisee.

The Act frequently refers to the position which would have obtained if the third party had been a party to the contact. Sub-section (4) clarifies this so that the third party should not be treated as a party to the contract for the purposes of any other Act. For example, Section 3 of the Unfair Contract Terms Act 1977 will not apply to third parties.

There is little point in giving rights to parties if they cannot be enforced. Rights can be enforced through the courts without difficulty. Increasingly, however in commercial situations, parties are looking to resolve their difficulties through arbitration. They have to do so by agreement, and the procedure is covered by an Act passed in 1996. The Arbitration Act 1996 was unusual in that it was not drafted by the Parliamentary Counsel who are responsible for most of the legislation – private and public – on the statute books, but by practising lawyers.

Arbitration

Its objectives are set out in Section 1. One of them is that parties should be free to agree how their disputes are resolved, subject only to such safeguards as are necessary in the public interest. There was no reason not to extend this principle to third parties. The effect, however, is different from the rest of the Act as it would not be right for a third party to be able to invoke arbitration proceedings or alternatively to go to Court as he wished, putting him in a better position than the promisee. Section 8 deals with this problem and provides that

8(1) *Where:-*

(a) a right under section 1 to enforce a term ("the substantive term") is subject to a term providing for the submission of disputes to arbitration ("the arbitration agreement") and

(b) the arbitration agreement is an agreement in writing for the purposes of Part I of the Arbitration Act 1996, the third party shall be treated for the purposes of that Act as a party to the arbitration agreement as regards disputes between himself and the promisor relating to the enforcement of the substantive term by the third party.

(2) Where:

(a) a third party has a right under section 1 to enforce a term providing for one or more

descriptions of dispute between the third party and the promisor to be submitted to arbitration ("the arbitration agreement").

(b) the arbitration agreement is an agreement in writing for the purposes of Part I of the Arbitration Act 1996, and

(c) the third party does not fall to be treated under subsection (1) as a party to the arbitration agreement, the third party shall, if he exercises the right, be treated for the purposes of that Act as a party to the arbitration agreement in relation to the matter with respect to which the right is exercised, and be treated as having been so immediately before the exercise of the right.

The third party is therefore required to submit to arbitration if this is provided for in the contract. This conditional benefit approach is the exception to the principle that the third party does not become subject to the burdens of the contract. The rationale is obvious.

Sub-section (2) deals with the comparatively rare situations where the conditional benefit approach is not applicable. The parties to a contact may give the third party a unilateral right to arbitrate or a right to arbitrate a dispute arising in connection with a right conferred on him. The effect of the sub-section is that this should be binding on the party only if he seeks to exercise that right.

Section 9 deals with the application of the Act to Northern Ireland. Section 10, the final section, sets out the title of the Act and provides when it is to come into force. These sections are set out in full in the Appendix.

Chapter 8

Conclusion

It is never easy to predict the effects of legislation. In the real world inhabited by businessmen and lawyers quite different imperatives are felt from those which drive the legislators. It has been argued for instance that legislation to protect tenants and borrowers has, because of market forces, frequently had the reverse affect from that intended. Moreover, the effects of legislation can change over time as its ramifications become better understood by the business community.

Nevertheless one thing is clear about the new Act. Contracts can be divided into those constituted by documents, which are consciously drawn up to be legally binding - frequently by lawyers - and those agreements which the law recognises as binding but which have not been consciously drafted. The former class which takes in most larger contracts is not likely to be greatly affected by the Act. Commercial contracts drafted by lawyers now increasingly contain a clause excluding the provisions of the Act. A lawyer advising a client entering into a contract will naturally try to limit the scope of his liability, preferably to the party with whom he is negotiating and who has given consideration for his promise. As a result the Act is hardly likely to revolutionise commercial life.

It is however the informal agreements at which the Act was principally directed. It is unlikely that ordinary people making arrangements without the benefit of legal advice will seek to limit their liability in relation to third parties. It is to be hoped therefore that cases like *Beswick -v- Beswick* which could on a literal interpretation of the law have created a terrible injustice will not recur. It must of course be remembered that legal commentators draw conclusions from the cases which comes to court.

In practice however forty nine cases out of fifty do not try but are settled by parties even if only at the door of the court. The settlements achieved are heavily influenced by the parties' perceptions of their chances if the case were to come to court. Hopefully now a third party in the position for instance of Mrs Beswick will get a better settlement than she could have obtained prior to the passing of the Act. In that case it will have achieved a great deal.

Appendix 1

Contracts (Rights of Third Parties) Act 1999

Contracts (Rights of Third Parties) Act 1999

Contracts (Rights of Third Parties)
Act 1999

1999 Chapter c.31

An Act to make provision for the enforcement of contractual terms by third parties.

[11th November 1999]

BE IT ENACTED by the Queen's most Excellent Majesty, by and with the advice and consent of the Lords Spiritual and Temporal, and Commons, in this present Parliament assembled, and by the authority of the same, as follows:-

Right of third party to enforce contractual term

1 1. - (1) Subject to the provisions of this Act, a person who is not a party to a contract (a "third party") may in his own right enforce a term of the contract if-

(a) the contract expressly provides that he may, or

(b) subject to subsection (2), the term purports to confer a benefit on him.

(2) Subsection (1)(b) does not apply if on a proper construction of the contract it appears that the parties did not intend the term to be enforceable by the third party.

(3) The third party must be expressly identified in the contract by name, as a member of a class or as answering a particular description but need not be in existence when the contract is entered into.

(4) This section does not confer a right on a third party to enforce a term of a contract otherwise than subject to and in accordance with any other relevant terms of the contract.

(5) For the purpose of exercising his right to enforce a term of the contract, shall be available to the third party any remedy that would have been available to him in an action for breach of contract if he had been a party to the contract (and the rules relating to damages, injunctions, specific performance and other relief shall apply accordingly).

(6) Where a term of a contract excludes or limits liability in relation to any matter references in this Act to the third party enforcing the term shall be construed as references to his availing himself of the exclusion or limitation.

(7) In this Act, in relation to a term of a contract which is enforceable by a third party-

"the promisor" means the party to the contract against whom the term is enforceable by the third party, and

"the promisee" means the party to the contract by whom the term is enforceable against the promisor.

(4) Where the consent of a third party is required under subsection (1) or (3), the court or arbitral tribunal may, on the application of the parties to the contract, dispense with his consent if satisfied-

(a) that his consent cannot be obtained because his whereabouts cannot reasonably be ascertained, or

(b) that he is mentally incapable of giving his consent.

(5) The court or arbitral tribunal may, the application of the parties to a contract, dispense with any consent that may be required under subsection (1)(c) if satisfied that it cannot reasonably be ascertained whether or not the third party has in fact relied on the term.

(6) If the court or arbitral tribunal dispenses with a third party's consent, it may impose such conditions as it thinks fit, including a condition requiring the payment of compensation to the third party.

(7) The jurisdiction conferred on the court by subsections (4) to (6) is exercisable by both the High Court and a county court.
(7) The jurisdiction conferred on the court by subsections (4) to (6) is exercisable by both the High Court and a county court.

Defences etc. available to promisor.

3 - (1) Subsections (2) to (5) apply where, in reliance on section 1, proceedings for the enforcement of a term of a contract are brought by a third party.

(2) The promisor shall have available to him by way of defence or set-off any matter that-

(a) arises from or in connection with the contract and is relevant to the term, and

(b) would have been available to him by way of defence or set-off if the proceedings had been brought by the promisee.

(b) it would have been available to him by way of defence or set-off if the proceedings had been brought by the promisee.

(4) The promisor shall also have available to him-

(a) by way of defence or set-off any matter, and

(b) by way of counterclaim any matter not arising from the contract,

that would have been available to him by way of defence or set-off or, as the case may be, by way of counterclaim against the third party if the third party had been a party to the contract.

(5) Subsections (2) and (4) are subject to any express term of the contract as to the matters that are not to be available to the promisor by way of defence, set-off or counterclaim.

(6) Where in any proceedings brought against him a third party seeks in reliance on section 1 to enforce a term of a contract (including, in particular, a term purporting to exclude or limit liability), he may not do so if he could not have done so (whether by reason of any particular circumstances relating to him or otherwise) had he been a party to the contract.

Enforcement of contract by promisee.

4 Section 1 does not affect any right of the promisee to enforce any term of the contract.

Protection of promisor from double liability.

5 Where under section 1 a term of a contract is enforceable by a third party, and the promisee has recovered from the promisor a sum in respect of-

(a) the third party's loss in respect of the term, or

(b) the expense to the promisee of making good to the third party the default of the promisor, then, in any proceedings brought in reliance on that section by the third party, the court or arbitral tribunal shall reduce any award to the third party to such extent as it thinks appropriate to take account of the sum recovered by the promisee.

Exceptions.

6 - (1) Section 1 confers no rights on a third party in the case of a contract on a bill of exchange, promissory note or other negotiable instrument.

(2) Section 1 confers no rights on a third party in the case of any contract binding on a company and its members under section 14 of the Companies Act 1985.

(3) Section 1 confers no right on a third party to enforce-

(a) any term of a contract of employment against an employee,

(b) any term of a worker's contract against a worker (including a home worker), or

(c) any term of a relevant contract against an agency worker.

(4) In subsection (3)-

(a) "contract of employment", "employee", "worker's contract", and "worker" have the meaning given by section 54 of the National Minimum Wage Act 1998,

(b) "home worker" has the meaning given by section 35(2) of that Act,

(c) "agency worker" has the same meaning as in section 34(1) of that Act, and

(d) "relevant contract" means a contract entered into, in a case where section 34 of that Act applies, by the agency worker as respects work falling within subsection (1)(a) of that section.

(5) Section 1 confers no rights on a third party in the case of-

(a) a contract for the carriage of goods by sea, or

(b) a contract for the carriage of goods by rail or road, or for the carriage of cargo by air, which is subject to the rules of the appropriate international transport convention, except that a third party may in reliance on that section avail himself of an exclusion or limitation of liability in such a contract.

(6) In subsection (5) "contract for the carriage of goods by sea" means a contract of carriage-

(a) contained in or evidenced by a bill of lading, sea waybill or a corresponding electronic transaction, or

(b) under or for the purposes of which there is given an undertaking which is contained in a ship's delivery order or a corresponding electronic transaction.

(7) For the purposes of subsection (6)-

(a) "bill of lading", "sea waybill" and "ship's delivery order" have the same meaning as in the Carriage of Goods by Sea Act 1992, and

(b) a corresponding electronic transaction is a transaction within section 1(5) of that Act which corresponds to the issue, indorsement, delivery or transfer of a bill of lading, sea waybill or ship's delivery order.

(8) In subsection (5) "the appropriate international transport convention" means-

(a) in relation to a contract for the carriage of goods by rail, the Convention which has the force of law in the United Kingdom under section 1 of the International Transport Conventions Act 1983,

(b) in relation to a contract for the carriage of goods by road, the Convention which has the force of law in the United Kingdom under section 1 of the Carriage of Goods by Road Act 1965, and

(c) in relation to a contract for the carriage of cargo by air-

(i) the Convention which has the force of law in the United Kingdom under section 1 of the Carriage by Air Act 1961, or

(ii) the Convention which has the force of law under section 1 of the Carriage by Air (Supplementary Provisions) 1962, or

(iii) either of the amended Conventions set out in Part B of Schedule 2 or 3 to the Carriage by Air Acts (Application of Provisions) Order 1967.

Supplementary provisions relating to third party.

7 - (1) Section 1 does not affect any right or remedy of a third party that exists or is available apart from this Act.

(2) Section 2(2) of the Unfair Contract Terms Act 1977 (restriction on exclusion etc. of liability for negligence) shall not apply where the negligence consists of the breach of an obligation arising from a term of a contract and the person seeking to enforce it is a third party acting in reliance on section 1.

(3) In sections 5 and 8 of the Limitation Act 1980 the references to an action founded on a simple contract and an action upon a specialty shall

respectively include references to an action brought in reliance on section 1 relating to a simple contract and an action brought in reliance on that section relating to a specialty.

(4) A third party shall not, by virtue of section 1(5) or 3(4) or (6), be treated as a party to the contract for the purposes of any other Act (or any instrument made
under any other Act).

Arbitration provisions.

8 - (1) Where-

(a) a right under section 1 to enforce a term ("the substantive term is subject to a term providing for the submission of disputes to arbitration ("the arbitration agreement"), and

(b) the arbitration agreement is an agreement in writing for the purposes of Part I of the Arbitration Act 1996, the third party shall be treated for the purposes of that Act as a party to the arbitration agreement as regards disputes between himself and the promisor relating to the enforcement of the substantive term by the third party.

Northern Ireland. 9 - (1) In its application to Northern Ireland, this Act has effect with the modifications specified in subsections (2) and (3).

(2) In section 6(2), for "section 14 of the Companies Act 1985" there is substituted "Article 25 of the Companies (Northern Ireland) Order 1986".

(3) In section 7, for subsection (3) there is substituted-

"(3) In Articles 4(a) and 15 of the Limitation (Northern Ireland) Order 1989, the references to an action founded on a simple contract and an action upon an instrument under seal shall respectively include references to an action brought in reliance on section 1 relating to a simple contract and an action brought in reliance on that section relating to a contract under seal.".

(4) In the Law Reform (Husband and Wife) (Northern Ireland) Act 1964, the following provisions are hereby repealed-

(a) section 5, and

(b) in section 6, in subsection (1)(a), the words "in the case of section 4" and "and in the case of section 5 the contracting party" and, subsection (3), the words "or section 5".

Short title, the commencement and extent.

10 - (1) This Act may be cited as Contracts (Rights of Third Parties) Act 1999.

(2) This Act comes into force on the day on which it is passed but, subject to subsection (3), does not apply in relation to a contract entered into before the end of the period of six months beginning with that day.

(3) The restriction in subsection (2) does not apply in relation to a contract which-

(a) is entered into on or after the day on which this Act is passed, and

(b) expressly provides for the application of this Act.

(4) This Act extends as follows-

(a) section 9 extends to Northern Ireland only;

(b) the remaining provisions extend to England and Wales and Northern Ireland only.

Appendix 2

Explanatory Notes to the Contracts (Rights of Third Parties) Act 1999

Explanatory Notes to Contracts (Rights Of Third Parties) Act 1999

1999 Chapter 31

These notes refer to the Contracts (Rights of Third Parties) Act 1999 which received Royal Assent on 11 November 1999 (c.31)

Contracts (Rights Of Third Parties) Act 1999

EXPLANATORY NOTES

INTRODUCTION

1. These explanatory notes relate to the Contracts (Rights of Third Parties) Act 1999 which received Royal Assent on 11 November 1999. They have been prepared by the Lord Chancellor's Department in order to assist the reader in understanding the Act. They do not form part of the Act and have not been endorsed by Parliament.

2. The notes need to be read in conjunction with the Act. They are not, and are not meant to be, a comprehensive description of the Act. So where a section or part of a section does not seem to require any explanation or comment, none is given.

SUMMARY

3. The Act reforms the rule of "privity of contract" under which a person can only enforce a contract if he is a party to it. The rule means that, even if a contract is made with the purpose of conferring a benefit on someone who is not a party to it, that person (a "third party") has no right to sue for breach of contract.

4. The Act sets out the circumstances in which a third party is to have a right to enforce a term of the contract (section 1), the situations in which such a term may be varied or rescinded (section 2) and the defences available to the promisor when the third party seeks to enforce the term (section 3). It makes it clear that section 1 does not affect the promisee's rights, or any rights that the third party may have which are independent of the Act (sections 4 and 7(1)). The Act does not apply to certain contracts (whether wholly or partially) (section 6).

BACKGROUND

5. The Act implements, with some amendments, the recommendations of the Law Commission in its Report on *Privity of Contract: Contracts for the Benefit of Third Parties*, Law Com No 242 (1996).

COMMENTARY

Section 1: Right of third party to enforce contractual term

6. *Section 1* gives effect to the central purpose of the Act. It sets out the circumstances in which a third party would have the right to enforce a term of the contract.

7. *Subsection (1)* sets out a two-limbed test for the circumstances in which a third party may enforce a term of a contract. The first limb is where the contract itself expressly so provides. The second limb is where the term purports to confer a benefit on the third party unless it appears on a true construction of the contract that the

contracting parties did not intend him to have the right to enforce it (*subsection (2)*).

8. *Subsection (3)* requires that, for subsection (1) to apply, the third party must be expressly identified in the contract by name, class or description, but establishes that the third party need not be in existence when the contract is made. This allows contracting parties to confer enforceable rights on, for example, an unborn child or a future spouse or a company that has not yet been incorporated.

9. *Subsection (4)* clarifies subsection (1). The third party's right of enforcement is subject to the contract's terms and conditions. It is open to the parties to limit or place conditions on the third party's right; for example, if he wishes to enforce the right he is to do so by way of arbitration and not litigation.

10. *Subsection (5)* makes it clear that the courts may award all the remedies which are available to a person bringing a claim for breach of contract to a third party seeking to enforce his rights under subsection (1). The normal rules of law applicable to those remedies, including the rules relating to causation, remoteness and the duty to mitigate one's loss, apply to the third party's claim.

11. *Subsection (6)* makes it clear that the Act is to apply so as to enable a third party to take advantage of an exclusion or limitation clause in the contract, as well as to enforce "positive" rights. The Act, for example, allows a term of a contract which excludes or limits the promisee's liability to the promisor for the tort of negligence and expressly states that the exclusion or limitation is for the benefit of the promisee's "agents or servants or subcontractors" to be enforceable by these groups.

Section 2: Variation and rescission of contract

12. *Subsection (1)* provides that, where a third party has a right under section 1, the contracting parties may not, by agreement, rescind or vary the contract in a way which affects the third party's right without his consent. This

section uses the term variation in its legal sense to mean a variation of the terms of an agreement by further agreement between the parties to the original agreement. It does not, for example, affect the terms of a construction contract which allow one of the parties to that contract unilaterally to alter, or "vary", the details of the work; such a variation is not to the contract but only to the work.

13. *Subsection (3)* provides that subsection (1) is subject to an express term of the contract, that the contract can by agreement be rescinded or varied without the third party's consent or that the third party's consent is to be required in specified circumstances different to those which are set out in subsection (1).

14. *Subsections (4) and (5)* give the court or arbitral tribunal the power to dispense with the requirement for the **third** party's consent where it cannot be obtained because his whereabouts are unknown or he is mentally incapable of giving his consent or where it cannot reasonably be ascertained whether he has in fact relied on the contractual term.

Section 3: Defences etc. available to promisor

15. *Section 3* enables the promisor, in a claim by the third party, to rely on any defence or set-off arising out of the contract and relevant to the term being enforced, which would have been available to him had the claim been by the promisee. He may also rely on any defence or set-off, or make any counterclaim, where this would have been possible had the third party been a party to the contract.

16. *Subsection (2)* can be illustrated as follows-

> (I) a third party can no more enforce a void, discharged or unenforceable contract than a promisee could;
>
> (II) P1 (the promisor) and P2 (the promisee) contract that P2 will sell goods to P1, who will pay the contract price to P3 (the third party). In breach of contract, P2 delivers goods that are not

> of the standard contracted for. In an action for the price by P3 (just as in an action for the price by P2) P1 is entitled to reduce or extinguish the price by reason of the damages for breach of contract.

17. *Subsection (3)* can be illustrated as follows-

> P1 and P2 contract that P1 will pay P3 if P2 transfers his car to P1. P2 owes P1 money under a wholly unrelated contract. P1 and P2 agree to an express term in the contract which provides that P1 can raise against a claim by P3 any matter which would have given P1 a defence or set-off to a claim by P2.

18. *Subsection (4)* makes it clear that the promisor also has available any defence or set-off, and any counterclaim not arising from the contract, which is specific to the third party. It can be illustrated as follows.

> (I) P1 contracts with P2 to pay P3 £1000. P3 already owes P1 £600. P1 has a set-off to P3's claim so that P1 is only bound to pay P3 £400.
>
> (II) P3 induced P1 to enter into the contract with P2 by misrepresentation, but P2 has no actual or constructive notice of that misrepresentation. P1 may have a defence (or a counterclaim for damages) against P3 which would not have been available had the action been brought by P2.

19. *Subsection (5)* makes subsections (2) and (4) subject to any express term of the contract which narrows the defences or set-offs available under section 3(2) or narrows the defences, set-offs or counterclaims available under section 3(4). For example-

> (I) in relation to subsection (2), P2 agrees with P1 to purchase a painting, the painting to be delivered to P3, who is expressly given a right to enforce the delivery obligation. P2 owes P1 considerable sums for other art works purchased. P2 wishes to ensure that P3's right is not affected. P1 and P2 expressly

agree that P1 may not raise against P3 defences and set-offs that would have been available to P1 in an action by P2.

(II) in relation to subsection (4), P1 agrees with P2 to pay £5000 to P3 if P2 will transfer a number of cases of wine to P1. P3 is in dispute with P1 over a prior contract and P1 alleges that P3 owes P1 money. P2 is concerned that P1 may seek to withhold part of the £5000 payable to P3 by raising a set-off or counterclaim against P3 in relation to the prior contract. Consequently P1 and P2 include an express term that P1 may raise no defences, set-offs or counterclaims of any nature whatever against a claim by P3 to enforce P1's obligation to pay the £5000.

20. *Subsection (6)* ensures that an analogous approach to that set out in subsections (2) to (5) applies where the proceedings are brought against the third party and he seeks to avail himself of, for example, an exclusion section.

Section 4: Enforcement of Contract by Promisee

21. *Section 4* provides that the right conferred by section 1 is additional to any right the promisee has in relation to the enforcement of a contract term which benefits a **third** party.

Section 5: Protection of Promisor from Double Liability

22. *Section 5* provides that where the promisee has recovered damages (or an agreed sum) from the promisor in respect of either the third party's loss or the promisee's expense in making good that loss, the court or arbitral tribunal shall reduce any award to the third party enforcing a term under section 1 to take account of the sum already recovered.

Section 6: Exceptions

23. *Subsection (1)* ensures that the Act does not undermine the existing law on who can enforce negotiable instruments.

24. *Subsection (2)* excepts the contract under section 14(1) of the Companies Act 1985 which states-

> "Subject to the provisions of this Act, the memorandum and articles, when registered, bind the company and its members to the same extent as if they respectively had been signed and sealed by each member, and contained covenants on the part of each member to observe all the provisions of the memorandum and of the articles".

25. *Subsection (3),* which prevents a third party (for example, a customer of an employer) acquiring a right under the Act to enforce a term of a contract of employment, or similar contract, against an employee or worker uses various expressions which are defined in the National Minimum Wage Act 1998 or are defined by reference to that Act. The definitions, which are referred to in *subsection (4)*, are as follows.

> (I) By section 54-
>
> "*contract of employment*" means a contract of service or apprenticeship, whether express or implied, and (if it is express) whether oral or in writing;
>
> "*employee*" means an individual who has entered into or works under (or, where the employment has ceased, worked under) a contract of employment;
>
> "*worker*" (except in the phrase "*agency worker*" or "*home worker*") means an individual who has entered into or works under (or, where the employment has ceased, worked under)-

(a) a *contract of employment*, or

(b) any other contract, whether express or implied and (if it is express) whether oral or in writing, whereby the individual undertakes to do or perform personally any work or services for another party to the contract whose status is not by virtue of the contract that of a client or customer of any profession or business undertaking carried on by the individual;

"*worker's contract*" is to be read in accordance with the definition of a worker.

(II) By section 35(2)-

an individual is a "*home worker*" if he contracts with a person for the purpose of that person's business, for the execution of work to be done in a placc not under the control or management of that person.

(III) By section 34(1)-

an individual is an "*agency worker*" if he-

(a) is supplied by a person ("the agent") to do work for another ("the principal") under a contract or other arrangements made between the agent and the principal; but

(b) is not, as respects that work, a worker, because of the absence of a worker's contract between the person and the agent or the principal; and

(c) is not a party to a contract under which he undertakes to do the work for another party to the contract whose status is, by virtue of the contract, that of a client or customer of any profession or business undertaking carried on by the individual.

(IV) As to the definition of "*relevant contract*", the reference to the case where section 34 applies is to the circumstances in which, under subsection (1) of that section, an individual is an agency worker. The work falling within paragraph (a) of that subsection is the work which the agency worker is supplied to do for the principal.

26. *Subsection (5),* which excludes certain contracts relating to the carriage of goods, nevertheless does not prevent a third party from taking advantage of a term excluding or limiting liability. In particular, this enables clauses which seek to extend an exclusion or limitation of liability of a carrier of goods by sea to servants, agents and independent contractors engaged in the loading and unloading process, to be enforced by those servants, agents or independent contractors (so called "Himalaya" clauses).

27. *Subsections (6) and (7)* set out the definition of a "contract for the carriage of goods by sea". The purpose of this definition is to exclude from this Act not only those contracts already covered by the Carriage of Goods by Sea Act 1992 but also those to which the 1992 Act could be applied under section 1(5) of that Act (e.g. a contract for the carriage of goods by sea evidenced by an electronic Act of lading). Section 1(5) of the 1992 Act states-

> "The Secretary of State may by regulations make provision for the application of this Act to cases where a telecommunication system or any other information technology is used for effecting transactions corresponding to -
>
> > (a) the issue of a document to which this Act applies;
> >
> > (b) the indorsement, delivery or other transfer of such a document; or
> >
> > (c) the doing of anything else in relation to such a document."

No such regulations have yet been made.

Section 7: Supplementary provisions relating to third party

28. *Subsection (1)* ensures that the Act does not affect any existing right or remedy of the third party and allows for the judicial development of a third party's rights.

29. *Subsection (2)* prevents a third party from invoking section 2(2) of the Unfair Contract Terms Act 1977 to contest the validity of a term excluding or limiting the promisor's liability under the Act to the third party for negligently caused loss or damage (other than personal injury or death). Section 2(2) of the 1977 Act (in which "other loss or damage" means loss or damage other than death or personal injury), states-

> "In the case of other loss or damage, a person cannot so exclude or restrict his liability for negligence except in so far as the term or notice satisfies the requirement of reasonableness".

30. *Subsection (3)*, which applies the standard limitation periods for actions for breach of contract to actions by third parties under the Act, refers to sections 5 and 8(1) of the Limitation Act 1980. Section 5 states-

> "An action founded on simple contract shall not be brought after the expiration of six years from the date on which the cause of action accrued".
>
> Section 8(1) states-
>
> "An action upon a specialty shall not be brought after the expiration of twelve years from the date on which the cause of action accrued".

31. *Subsection (4)* ensures that those references in the Act to the position "if the third party had been a party to the contract" are not to be interpreted as meaning that the third party should be treated as a party to the contract for the purposes of any other enactment. One example is section 3 of the Unfair Contract Terms Act 1977 which applies "as between contracting parties where one of them deals as a consumer or on the other's written standard terms

of business". This subsection makes it clear that nothing in sections 1(5) or 3(4) or 3(6) means that "contracting parties" in section 3 of the 1977 Act includes a third party with a right under section 1 of this Act.

32. Nothing in subsection (4), nor anything in paragraphs 13.1-13.8 of the Law Commission's Report (*Privity of Contract: Contracts for the Benefits of Third Parties*, Law Com. Report No. 242), is intended to have any bearing on the interpretation of Article 17 of the Brussels Convention (on jurisdiction agreements). This is given effect to in the United Kingdom by the Civil Jurisdiction and Judgments Act 1982. The question of whether a third party given a procedural right to enforce a jurisdiction agreement under section 1 of this Act falls within Article 17, or whether a third party with a substantive right under section 1, subject to a jurisdiction clause, is "bound" by that clause under Article 17 (applying a conditional benefit analysis) is a matter for the European Court of Justice. Relevant decisions of the ECJ include *Gerling v il Tesoro* [1983] ECR 2503 and *Tilly Russ* [1984] ECR 2417.

Section 8: Arbitration provisions

33. *Section 8* ensures that, where appropriate, the provisions of the Arbitration Act 1996 apply in relation to third party rights under this Act. Without this section, the main provisions of the Arbitration Act 1996 would not apply because a third party is not a party to the arbitration agreement between the promisor and the promisee.

34. *Subsection (1)* deals with what is likely to be the most common situation. The third party's substantive right (for example, to payment by the promisor) is conferred subject to disputes being referred to arbitration (see section 1(4)). This section is based on a "conditional benefit" approach. It ensures that a third party who wishes to take action to enforce his substantive right is not only able to enforce effectively his right to arbitrate, but is also "bound" to enforce his right by arbitration (so that, for example, a stay of proceedings can be ordered against him under

section 9 of the Arbitration Act 1996). This approach is analogous to that applied to assignees who may be prevented from unconscionably taking a substantive benefit free of its procedural burden (see, for example, *DVA v Voest Alpine, The Jaybola* [1997] 2 Lloyd's Rep 279). "Disputes .... relating to the enforcement of the substantive term by the third party" is intended to have a wide ambit and to include disputes between the third party (who wishes to enforce the term) and the promisor as to the validity, interpretation, existence or performance of the term; the third party's entitlement to enforce the term; the jurisdiction of the arbitral tribunal; or the recognition and enforcement of an arbitration award. But to avoid imposing a "pure" burden on the third party, it does not cover, for example, a separate dispute in relation to a tort claim by the promisor against the third party for damages.

35. *Subsection (2)* is likely to be of rarer application. It deals with situations where the third party is given a right to arbitrate under section 1 but the "conditional benefit" approach underpinning subsection (1) is inapplicable. For example, where the contracting parties give the third party a unilateral right to arbitrate or a right to arbitrate a dispute other than one concerning a right conferred on the third party under section (1). To avoid imposing a pure burden on the third party (in a situation where, for example, the contracting parties give the third party a right to arbitrate a tort claim made by the promisor against the third party) the subsection requires the third party to have chosen to exercise the right. The timing point at the end of the subsection is designed to ensure that a third party who chooses to exercise his right to go to arbitration by, for example, applying for a stay of proceedings under section 9 of the Arbitration Act 1996, can do so. Under section 9 of the Arbitration Act 1996, the right to apply for a stay of proceedings can only be exercised by someone who is already a party to the arbitration agreement.

Section 9: Northern Ireland

36. *Section 9* modifies the Act in its application to Northern Ireland and makes consequential repeals in existing Northern Ireland legislation.

37. *Subsection (2)* modifies section 6(2) so that, in Northern Ireland, it has effect with a reference to the Northern Ireland equivalent of section 14 of the Companies Act 1985. This is Article 25(1) of the Companies (Northern Ireland) Order 1986, which states-

> "Subject to the provisions of this Order, the memorandum and articles, when registered, bind the company and its members to the same extent as if they respectively had been signed and sealed by each member, and contained covenants on the part of each member to observe all the provisions of the memorandum and of the articles."

38. *Subsection (3)* modifies section 7 so that, in Northern Ireland, subsection (3) refers in appropriate terms to the Northern Ireland equivalents of sections 5 and 8 of the Limitation Act 1980. These are Articles 4(a) and 15 of the Limitation (Northern Ireland) Order 1989. Article 4(a) provides that an action founded on simple contract may not be brought after the expiration of six years from the date on which the cause of action accrued. Article 15 provides that an action upon an instrument under seal may not be brought after the expiration of 12 years from the date on which the cause of action accrued.

39. *Subsection (4)* repeals section 5 of the Law Reform (Husband and Wife) (Northern Ireland) Act 1964. This section modifies the rule of privity of contract in respect of contracts which are expressed to be for the benefit of, or expressly purport to confer a right on, the spouse or child of one of the contracting parties. As this Act makes comprehensive provision for third party beneficiaries under a contract, there is no longer any need for this provision. Subsection (4) also makes repeals in section 6 of the Law Reform (Husband and Wife) (Northern Ireland)

Act 1964 Act which are consequential on the repeal of section 5 of that Act.

APPLICATION TO THE CROWN

40. This Act does not impose any obligation or restraint on the Crown. It is simply an enabling measure which allows the parties to a contract, including the Crown, to confer enforceable rights on third parties. The Crown Proceedings Act 1947 enables proceedings in contract to be brought against the Crown, whether they are brought by the promisee or a third party.

COMMENCEMENT

41. The Act is to come into force on Royal Assent (section 10). It will only apply to contracts which are entered into during the six month period after Royal Assent if the contract expressly provides for it to do so. Where there is no such express provision it will not apply to contracts entered into before the end of that six month period.

HANSARD REFERENCES

42. The following table sets out the dates and Hansard references for each stage of this Act's passage through Parliament.

Stage

Date

Hansard Reference

House of Lords

Introduction	3 December 1998	Vol. 595 Col. 605
Second Reading	11 January 1999	Vol. 596 Cols. 20-33
Committee	2 February 1999	Vol. 596 Cols. 1423-35
Report	27 May 1999	Vol. 601 Cols. 1046-1061

Third Reading 14 June 1999 Vol. 602 Cols. 11-14

House of Commons

Introduction 14 June 1999 -

Second Reading Committee 29 June 1999

Second Reading Committee Hansard

Second Reading (formal) 5 July 1999 Vol. 334 Col. 791

Committee (SCF) 15 July 1999

Standing Committee D Hansard

Report/Third Reading 1 November 1999

Vol. 337 Cols. 23-30

House of Lords

Consideration of Commons Amendments 10 November 1999 Vol. 606 Cols. 1361-1366

Royal Assent - 11 November 1999

House of Lords

House of Commons

Hansard Vol. 606 Col 1469

Hansard Vol. 337 Col 1306

APPENDIX 3

Summary of Cases

1678 ***Dutton -v- Poole* 2 Law 210: 83 tR523**

A son promised his father that in return for the father's not selling a wood which he owned the sun would pay £1,000 to his sister. The son failed to pay whereupon the sister sued. She was successful even though the promise was not made to her but to her father.

1812 ***Phillips -v- Bateman* 16 East 356, 371 104 ER 1124**

Facing a run on a bank A. agreed to support it with £30,000 whereupon the bank's noteholders stopped withdrawing their money. Later the bank failed. A. was held not liable in an action by the noteholders.

1823 ***Carnegie -v- Waugh* 1 LJ (OS) KB 89**

Tutors and curators of an infant entered into an agreement for lease requiring a rent to be paid to the infant. It was held that the agreement was enforceable by the infant even though not a party to it.

1861 ***Tweddle -v- Atkinson* 1 B&S 393**

The fathers of a bride and groom agreed before the wedding that the father of the bride would pay a sum of money to the groom. The groom subsequently sued the father's estate for this sum. He failed as he was not party to the agreement.

Eurymedon

1974 ***The New Zealand Shipping Co Ltd -v- A M Salterthwaite & Co Ltd: the Eurymedon 1 A.E.R. 1015.***

An independent contractor acting as a stevedore for a carrier negligently damaged the owner's cargo. The contractor sought to rely on a clause in the carrier's contract with the owner exempting the carrier and his agents from any liability for negligence. They were successful.

1967 ***Beswick -v- Beswick* [1967] 2AER 1997**

Mr Beswick carried on a coal business in partnership with his nephew. He agreed to sell the business to his nephew on the basis that his nephew would pay him an annuity for the rest of his life and following his death would pay a reduced annuity to his widow. The nephew paid the annuity until Mr Beswick Senior died but after making one payment he refused to pay Mrs Beswick. She sued and Mr Beswick Junior claimed that she was a stranger to the contract and therefore could not enforce it. The House of Lords accepted this but held that Mrs Beswick could enforce the contract in her capacity as an executrix of her husband's estate although she was unable to do so in her own capacity.

1975 ***Jackson -v- Horizon Holidays Limited*** **[1975] 2 AER 1992**

Mr Jackson booked a holiday for himself, his wife and his two children in Ceylon. The holiday turned out to be a disaster and the holiday company accepted they were in breach of contract. They argued however that Mrs Jackson and her children were strangers to the contract and therefore could not claim damages for its breach. The Court of Appeal found away round this by enabling Mr Jackson to recover for their loss on the basis that this spoiled his holiday.

1980 ***Woodar Investment Developments Limited -v- Wimpey Construction (UK) Limited*** **[1980] 1 AER 571**

The owners of 14 acres of land agreed to sell it on the basis that the buyer would pay £850,000 to them and on completion a further £150,000 to third parties having no connection with the sellers. On an action for breach of contract the buyers argued that even if they were liable for damages none should be recoverable by the third parties. This argument was successful in the House of Lords although the case did in fact turn on other issues.

GLOSSARY OF TERMS

Action: A civil case of any kind

Agreement: Contract. The terms are inter-changeable.

Arbitral Tribunal : Any body of one or more people carrying out an arbitration

Bill: A legislative proposal being considered by Parliament. Once a Bill has been passed and has received the Royal Assent it is known as an Act.

Claimant: Anyone bringing a civil action of any kind. Before the Woolf Reforms he was known as a ***plaintiff.***

Consideration: The quid pro quo which must be given for a promise under a contract. Consideration can consist of another promise or of an immediate action such as a cash payment.

Contract: An agreement between two or more people whereby they confer benefits on each other. In certain specialised areas such as the sale of land a contract must be in writing but under general law a contract need not be in writing and need not even be verbal. In certain circumstances a contract can even be inferred from conduct.

Counterclaim: A reply by a defendant to an action to the effect that regardless of the merits of the claimant's own claim, the claimant is liable to him for monies. Unlike set-off a counterclaim need not arise out of the same transaction as the original claim and can be for a greater sum.

Defence: Covers any argument raised by a defendant as to why he should not be liable to the claimant. In an action for breach of contract a defence could be to the effect that the contract had not been made at all, or, if it was made, it was not valid, or, if valid, it was not enforceable, or, if enforceable, it should not be enforced in this case e.g. because of the conduct of the claimant.

Defendant: The person against whom an action is brought. In an action for breach of contract the Defendant will frequently be the promisor.

Personal property: Property other than freehold land. It includes things in action.

Plaintiff: The old term for a ***claimant.***

Privity: Short for privity of contract. The rule that only a party to a contract could enforce it. By extension the term was also applied to an original tenant's liability throughout the term of his lease. In 1995 this principle was also abolished by Parliament.

Promisee: A person to whom a promise is made under a contract. The doctrine of privity meant that only the promisee could enforce the contract.

Promisor: The person making the promise under the contract.

Real property: Sometimes referred to as realty or real estate. It refers to freehold land. Leasehold land is understood by the law not to be real property but a contract and therefore personal property.

Set-off: Where a defendant argues that the claimant is liable to him for monies usually as a result of the same transaction. Where a defendant claims set-off the amount he seeks cannot exceed the amount of the claimant's claim.

Specific performance: An order by the Court requiring a party to carry out his obligations under a contract.

A thing in action: Often known by lawyers as a ***chose in action***. It confers on its owner not the enjoyment or use of a concrete object but a right which is enforceable in Court. Examples are contracts, debts and marketable securities such as stocks and shares.

Third Party: In relation to a contract, someone who is not a party to it but may be an intended beneficiary. For instance two commercial partners may make arrangements with each other for the benefit of their wives and children.

Tort: A general breach of duty. It can be owed to any number of people and is distinguished from contractual duties which arise only out of obligations which have been voluntarily assumed by the defendant.

Index

Appendix 1

Appendix 2

Appendix 3

Table of Cases

Table of Statutes